CONTENTS

3. Wilted flowers and faded memories
4. The Gardener
5. Seasons of life
6. Shattered dreams and broken promises.
7. Night and day
8. A rare bottled wine
9. I have to get dressed
10. Flattery
11. Room for success
12. There's a fly in my room
13. Good morning love
14. Think young man or at least try
15. Come in from out of the cold
16. I just know I can win
17. Water
18. Gather up the leaves
19. Corrupt words and sinful thoughts
20. The meadows
22. The magnolia tree
23. The long walk
24. O my beautiful black queen
25. The palm tree
26. Cotton sheets
27. Destiny
29. Caught up in a dream
30. Farewell my love
31. Mother me
32. Death
33. Unkind words
34. The kiss
35. A late bloomer
36. Special Quotes
43. What about life
44. Hardships
45. I love to hug you and hold you tight
47. Snow flakes in the winter
48. Words of wisdom
49. Frivolous talk

WILTED FLOWERS AND FADED MEMORIES

Wilted flowers and faded memories.

Where has life gone?

The ground where the soil lay has become hard and dry.

Once moistened by the rain water, but now forgotten and left to die.

Her soul drifting from reality and wrestling with sanity.

Canst thou remember anymore I said !

My lovely rose began to fade

And now the flower that was planted has withered away!

THE GARDENER

It was morning as I walked
through the garden

Breathing in the fresh air
and aroma of the flowers

An orchestra of colors
playing in the sunlight

Tulips, lilies, gardenias,
mums and roses

And I the gardener tending
to the concert of flowers

received a standing ovation
as others began to bloom!

SEASONS OF LIFE

Life is as the seasons change, all are different and none the same. Once the seed is planted we are born in the spring, fresh from our mother's womb! Our youth coming in summer's heat. We passed through puberty and became infatuated, later falling in love. For I am as strong as a stallion now and ready to run til autumn comes! It is then when life makes a sudden change. And in the winter when I am very old I soon will die !

SHATTERED DREAMS AND BROKEN PROMISES

Shattered dreams and broken promises, my love has gone from me. We did exchange vows, but now are separated from the years we were together. She is held captive by infidelity, and I chained to my feelings unable to get free. Jilted by memories and left standing at the altar waiting for my love to return !

NIGHT AND DAY

I stood beneath a blackened sky. The night was dreary, filled with emptiness and a lonely walk. Not aware of whence or where I had trodden. I only knew I was on this road before, but this time I will not continue until daybreak . I will wait until the clouds have awakened and the sun pushes through. When the birds have whistled in the morning dew as the snow covered mountains look on from a distance. Capturing a glimmer of hope from the light to follow. Then it will brighten the way for me to run and leap for joy as galloping horses !

A RARE BOTTLED WINE

She was young and I older. I only pick grapes when they have ripened, and she was for awhile. Not as aged wine yet good to taste. I found her in the vineyard fully grown, so I gathered her up into the basket of my heart. I had a crush on her, and the romance began at the harvest dance. A rare bottled wine placed on the top shelf. She is special to me, and I will allow no one to drink from my glass !

I HAVE TO GET DRESSED

I need you to help me get dressed

You are like the garment one wears and without you I am naked As one needing an umbrella in the rain or searching for shelter I like a tailored suit because it fits me well One sewn together with
the finest material

Weddings are formal and I need to have on the right apparel, so that when I walk down the aisle, I am walking with you !

FLATTERY

Please don't praise me with flattering words to arouse my suspicion, petting your cat to purr by your own admission. Let me be who I am without endorsing me to star in a play that's never been written. For I am by no means an actor!

ROOM FOR SUCCESS

My son success is waiting on you. I know you have failed and given up, *but wait* ! Failure is our teacher. It teaches us how to succeed. Have you learned anything yet? Why are you sitting in the basement, when there are other rooms upstairs? If I were you I would take steps to see the rest of the house. Success is just waiting to show you around !

THERE'S A FLY IN MY ROOM

Might I be concerned about the fly in my room. It may just leave, but that I can't assume. I refuse to go to sleep until I have swatted that fly or smashed it with the broom. For it's bound to land somewhere with those bulging eyes. I am greatly annoyed as it flies around seemingly confused. Darting in and out in so many directions. My eyes have grown tired trying to follow. Now I am as restless as the fly! Then through a hole in the screen the fly flew, and I was able to sleep the whole night through!

GOOD MORNING LOVE

Good morning love !

I never saw you fall asleep

How is it that your never tired

Your much different than the others I meet !

Got to get to know you better !

THINK YOUNG MAN OR AT LEAST TRY

You have become irrational
in your thinking

What is your reason
for not reasoning ?

Your thoughts are wayward and no
longer can understanding be found
in you

Now I am perplexed to say the
least at your lack of cognition

So think young man or at least try !

Listen, pay attention, seek to
comprehend

Don't allow knowledge to escape
you, but embrace it and yearn for it

For it will deliver you from
ignorance and prepare you for the
future

So think young man or at least try !

COME IN FROM OUT OF THE COLD

Come in from out of the cold

and let me hold you close
to my heart where it is warm

Let us shelter each other
from the rain

For nothing and no one
shall come between

this love that bonds us together

I JUST KNOW I CAN WIN

The gambler is always
determined to win.

He's compulsive, addictive,
and relying on chance

So roll the dice or lay
down your hand

And watch me try to win

I'll wager my house .
I'll wager my car

Without even realizing
I've gone too far

All I need is a room til
I get on my feet

I just know I can win if

the dealer doesn't cheat !

WATER

Rivers, oceans, ponds, and streams. Lakes, brooks, bays, and seas. Water is everywhere, and never is it depleted. Rain after rain, it saturates the earth's soil causing flowers to grow. The farmer plants his crop depending on it. My thirst is quenched and my body cleansed by it. Noah warned the people but they did not take heed, and the flood did destroy. So take me and sit me be down by tranquil waters that are still, away from the storm. To a place that quiets my soul and calms my spirit!

GATHER UP THE LEAVES

The leaves have fallen from the tree, and are scattered throughout the world. They are of many nations and various races. Come with me now to gather up the lost souls and rake in those who have strayed away. We are the branches connected to the Tree of Life, so let us gather up the leaves while there is still time !

CORRUPT WORDS AND SINFUL THOUGHTS

Corrupt words and sinful thoughts. Whether spoken or heard , that's saying a lot ! Vulgarity and Profanity are like untuned pianos and empty jars. A sound quite disturbing, irritating, and hard. Hardcore thoughts, perverted minds, filthy discussions and twisted vines. Latching on to the soul, unchallenged by purity and bold !

THE MEADOWS

A blanket of flowers had covered the meadows. They pushed their way up through the blades of grass, almost as if someone had arranged them. I found myself in the midst of a floral display tucked away in the mountains. A serene and peaceful dwelling away from the city. Only hearing the sound of a waterfall as it echoed the rushing waters. I knew that I was supposed to be there to enjoy the quietness and beauty of the fields. Then night fell and I lodged there til morning. Leaving to return home but staying behind the moment!

THE MAGNOLIA TREE

I could smell a sweet aroma coming from the magnolia tree. It grew to be very tall and her blossoms shielded me from the sun. I rested beneath the shade and leaned against her trunk. For she was a strong southern bell and her roots very deep !

THE LONG WALK

I walked down the road, layered with rock and gravel. My feet pigeon toed, I knew I had far to travel. My life had many bumps and turns. While on this road I was told I'd learn. So on down the road I went, hoping it would end. My legs now tired from when I first began. Then as I continued walking, I could hear my children play. My wife and neighbors talking, and I knew I was home to stay!

O MY BEAUTIFUL BLACK QUEEN

O my beautiful black Queen ! I searched all over for you, then you came. Pushed out from between the thighs of Africa and landing on American soil. Once a slave, but now free. Segregated and rejected, now elevated and respected. Your eyes aglow like stars in the night. Let me climb your fertile walls and hold you tight. Braided hair, a fro, or a weave. I'm locked in with you, not wanting to be free !

THE PALM TREE

I was on a beautiful island as the palm tree swayed back and forth. Amazed by its appeal of strength as it towered over me. Defiant to the storms, and standing its ground. For it had a sure foundation , attaching itself to the earth below. Like a brave soldier, it stood at attention and saluted the God of the universe !

COTTON SHEETS

Let me sleep awhile beneath my cotton sheets. I'm trying to get some rest you see, my mouth closed and gritting teeth. Tossing and turning, almost on the floor, I get tired of asking, just need a little more. Everytime I close my eyes, the phone rings. The lights are out, TV is off, did I miss anything ! Let me sleep awhile beneath these cotton sheets. I need to lay here a little longer, is that too hard to see!

DESTINY

I marched with destiny . I believed her when she guided me along as fate would have it. She became my designated future, reluctant to come to a halt, until I have reached my destination. For I was recruited by her and have fallen in place without missing a beat !

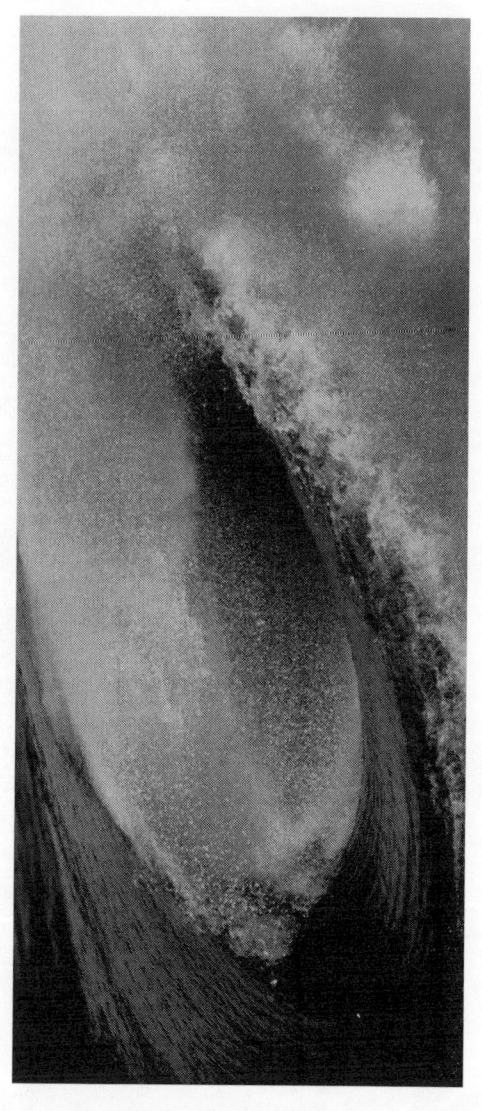

CAUGHT UP IN A DREAM

I was caught up in a dream. Though fearless as the waves rolled in, the howling wind roared at the sea. Twas only I on a ship moving over dangerous waters with no captain onboard. With no one to bother, I took the rudder and did take control. Riding the high tides in the midst of a storm. I became a castaway, left to die but still trusting in the Lord. Cold and sweating, I pushed back the sheets. Now awake from the dream while asleep !

FAREWELL MY LOVE

What shall I do with this love I have for you? Though it is pure, I am forbidden to have you, thus I must say adieu! I will not part with this love, but will not allow it to take me beyond the boundaries that contain us. Shall we respond to this love and covet happiness while others suffer ? Making things more complex, simply finding what we've discovered ! I will remain behind and let you go. You have my heart, so farewell my love, farewell !

MOTHER ME

Hold me close to thy bosom where

I will find warmth. Nourish me

with thy milk while I am still a

child. Mother me with thy love still

yet awhile. You did give birth to

me, and I will honor you when I

am old !

DEATH

I attended a funeral of a loved one with her casket on display. Tears along with whispers *it didn't have to end this way!* Death is surrounded by flowers, bright, fresh, and alive. As sorrow rain down showers, they too will fade and die !

UNKIND WORDS

Unkind words usually cause a stir.

Harshly spoken and painfully

heard. Never considered or given

much thought, abusive, disturbing,

and randomly brought !

THE KISS

I felt her lips pressed against mine as our eyes met. Intense emotions unwind with no regret. She knew my every thought, more than that which I had sought. A romance so strong we call our own. A kiss, a gentle touch, a sense of feeling secure. I reminisce not having enough, always wanting more!

A LATE BLOOMER

I was a late bloomer, as the flowers which blossom in the winter. God's gift to me was hiding in the shadows, but now is apparent for all to see. No longer do I stammer, but able to speak clearly. They doubted and now believe!

SPECIAL QUOTES

BY HERBERT NEWELL

If you value someone or something, make time your investment!

Worse than knowing something that you know is true, is the suspense of not knowing something that is said to be true !

False accusations can often be persuasive, depending on who is listening on the other end !

Like a volcano getting ready to erupt, is an angry man who holds a grudge !

Challenges are contests, always looking for a winner. Obstacles are challenges we must overcome !

A man's wealth is obtained through wisdom. How he spends it determines how long it will last !

WHAT ABOUT LIFE

What shall we do about life? It is not ours, but has been given to us . So what will we do with the life that has been given to us? As for me, I will live and share life with others and give them the hope that was given me through Christ. He is that hope that springeth forth as the daylight, dispelling all darkness !

HARDSHIPS

Don't weep for me, for I must endure this hardship to improve my character. Oddly enough, I have become more determined than less to allow it to happen. It will be helpful to me eventually. For had it not been, I would not know the joy to follow. Gain will be the outcome of my loss. Afterall, success is more valuable to me when I've first experienced failure!

I LOVE TO HUG YOU AND HOLD YOU TIGHT

I love to hug you and hold you tight, just because it feels right To go for a walk or sit down and talk, from morning to evening, throughout the night. To light a candle, to dine and dance, to bring you flowers every given chance. To run through the water, to splash and play or plan a picnic the entire day. So hug me and hold me tight, just because I know it feels so right!

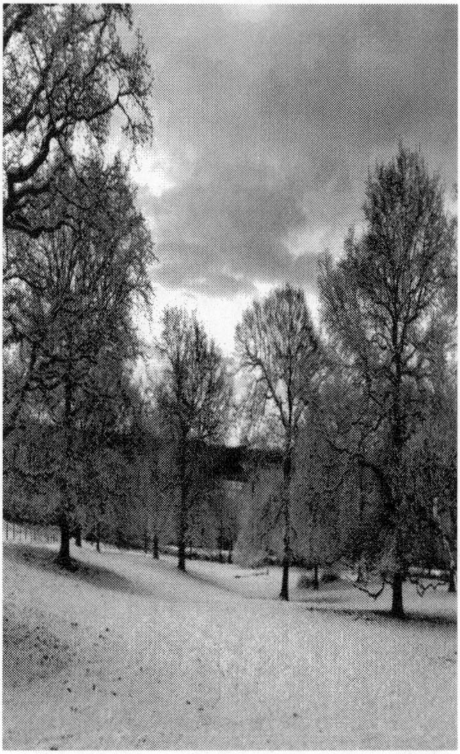

SNOW FLAKES IN THE WINTER

Night was brewing as evening

came, and the day about to end.

It was quiet and still through my

window pane, as flakes of snow

descend. Time paused for spring,

as winter settled in!

WORDS OF WISDOM

By Herbert Newell

When you are confronted about something, whether right or wrong, always respond in a mature manner!

Always be the owner of every decision you make, and don't let others influence you!

FRIVOLOUS TALK

Don't trouble me with frivolous talk. I haven't the time to waste my thoughts. Give me something to think about, to remember, or to try and comprehend. Ask me something I don't know, that way I can't pretend !

This book is dedicated to those who have experienced the mental loss of a loved one through Dementia. Dementia is a loss of mental skills that affects a person's daily life. It affects memory, thinking, language, judgment, behavior, and a person's ability to perform normal task. It can cause problems with a person's memory and how well they think and plan. As time progresses an individual diagnosed with Dementia begins to have "Faded Memories". For the loved ones of the diagnosed, the question remains the same, "How do I care for my loved one while respecting the life they lived and are still trying to hold onto?" I personally know of the suffering that families endure, as my mother was diagnosed with this disease. *Wilted flowers* indicate loss of life. As her memories faded, her life began to decline and finally she passed away. God gave me the strength I needed to get through it. He will do the same for you!

Herbert Newell

IN LOVING MEMORY OF MY MOM

I thank God for the gift He has given me. I pray that this book might uplift spirits and minister to people all over the world. Special thanks to Alexis Howard for her input and all those who have inspired me to write

                Herbert Newell